Nantwich

in old picture postcards

1880-1930

by
Allan Whatley

European Library – Zaltbommel/Netherlands

GB   ISBN 90 288 5380 4 CIP

© 1992 European Library – Zaltbommel/Netherlands

FOREWORD

This compilation owes its existence to searches made in four different collections of postcards: two held by collectors and two in public institutions.

The choice from some 500 postcards was difficult, partly to create a publication of views, etcetera, which have not already been published in other books, and partly, to meet the requirements of the publishers of the European Library, namely, to be within the timespan 1880-1930.

Fewer than half of the cards chosen carry the names of the publishers. Among them are fourteen different names.

In spite of having such a wide selection of postcards, it was disappointing to discover that relatively few postcards were produced which showed ordinary people going about their every-day pursuits. I might have seen fifty views of the parish church or as many of the Brine Baths Hotel but almost none had that vital 'human interest' element beloved of a good photographer. For this reason a few views appear here which have been used elsewhere.

I acknowledge with grateful thanks the big debt I owe to David Langford of Shavington near Nantwich for the opportunity to see his large collection and to use his postcards for the bulk of this book. A few others were borrowed from Sheila Kane, Librarian, Nantwich Library. My thanks to her too.

The approximate date of a postcard is shown in parentheses.

Nantwich, 1992   Allan Whatley

INTRODUCTION

In 1880 Nantwich was a small country town of about 7,500 inhabitants. By 1930 it had only 7,100. It was the local market town for the rural hinterland within a radius of ten miles. Dairying was the principal rural industry; cheese was regularly brought to Nantwich for sale or for dispatch by canal to Lancashire to the north or to the Midlands to the south. The first Cheese Fair was held in Nantwich in 1882 and is still a feature of the Nantwich Annual Show.

Nantwich stands on the river Weaver which flows northwards to join the Mersey. The town, which stretches for a mile along one main road (formerly the coaching road from London to Chester), is notable for the number of buildings which have survived from the sixteenth and seventeenth centuries. It has been designated a Conservation Town of historic interest.

Crewe, only four miles away, was an upstart town of the first half of the nineteenth century created with the arrival of the railway age as a focal point for several railway lines as well as locomotive engineering works.

The main source of work in Nantwich was still the boot- and shoemaking industry. Census figures for 1851 to 1881 show that there was a gradual decline in the number of workers in the leather industry after 1870 as bigger factories with bigger machines were opened in other parts of England. The decline continued until the last factory closed in 1932.

The mill on the Weaver had been spinning cotton up to 1876 but thereafter clothing factories were opened in the town and took over many of the workers from the boot and shoe industry. Several small clothing factories continue to this day. The census figures again show the change. The numbers of workers in the clothing trade were: 51 in 1851; 359 in 1871 and 674 in 1881.

There was a close link between town and country. People did not travel very far from their homes. The pace of life was geared to the movements of cattle to and from the market and the pace of horse-drawn vehicles.

Church and chapel occupied much of people's spare time. There were ten places of worship with St.Mary's parish church dominating the town centre. These religious organisations were responsible for the setting up of schools before compulsory elementary education was introduced in 1870. The sixteenth century grammar school was moved in 1860 to new premises and combined with a charity school. There were several private schools but these declined or closed as state schools took over. In 1892 the National School had 660 pupils and the Wesleyan Methodist school about 750. St. Mary's church acquired a new hall and meeting rooms in 1886.

From 1890 Technical Institute classes and university extension lectures were held in the parish hall. By 1902 a Technical Institute had been built to mark Queen Victoria's Diamond Jubilee in 1897.

Girls were admitted to the grammar school. As the school grew so more space was needed. A new school was erected in 1921 and by 1928 it had 250 pupils for secondary education.

Other notable buildings erected during the period include the following. To mark Queen Victoria's Golden Jubilee (fifty years' reign from 1837 to 1887) the people of Nantwich decided to erect a 'Free' or Public Library under the 1850-1855 Public Libraries Acts. It began with 5,000 books and stayed open until 10p.m. This was very successful in its early years but later fell below standard for lack of financial support which restricted a regular supply of new books. The theory was that the public library would draw people away from the public house. Much more likely to do this was the popular Cocoa House or The Three Cups which had moved its premises across Pillory Street into larger premises next door to the library. It began in 1879. Tea, coffee, cocoa or soup were served. Newspapers were provided and some board games were available. There was a room set aside for ladies and a Penny Bank operated. Poverty was a real threat; wages were low and ways of encouraging savings through penny banks, friendly societies and other banks were encouraged.

The Town Hall, near the site of the brine pit from which Nantwich owes its origin, was extended to accommodate a swimming bath and ten private medicinal brine baths. Some speculators felt that Nantwich might be turned into a spa town equal to those elsewhere in England or Germany. A scheme was launched to build a fine hotel on land to the south side of the town. As the postcard views show, it was a fine complex set in attractive surroundings. It too was successful for a period, 1892 to 1932, but unfortunately it did not make Nantwich famous as a spa town.

By 1900 some of the oldest parts of the town, perhaps pretty to look at as timber-framed, thatched cottages, were falling into disrepair or poor condition. So the first clearance, said to be a 'slum' clearance took place. No doubt memories of the great cholera epidemic of 1849 caused public health officials to take this action.

A Cottage Hospital was opened in 1907. In 1911 an imposing department-type store in decorative architectural style was erected on the corner site of Hospital Street and Pillory Street. Not many yards away, in the same year, the pseudo-timber-framed frontage for W.H.Smith & Son added to the attractive appearance of the Square. After the First World War 'Ye Olde Wyche Theatre' was built alongside the Market Hall. It was a cinema for many years.

Before the days when women were given the right to vote in elections, political views were fairly evenly divided between Conservative and Liberal persuasions. The period ended with the very important act of two civic-minded people who restored one of the town's gems: Churche's Mansion of 1577 just when it was about to fall into decay. That set an example for much more restoration and preservation in later years.

As well as church and chapel activities such as fêtes and outings, Nantwich people were keenly interested in musical events: choral, operatic, concerts, as well as dancing, football, cricket, tennis, bowling, poultry and cage bird exhibitions, dog racing, pigeon racing. There was always a lively welcome for touring fairs, performing animals, bands, or individual acts.

The first motor cars were seen in town in 1903. Thereafter the motor age arrived, at first vying with horse-drawn means of transport and then gradually superseding them. The days of street congestion were still a long way off.

Many shopkeepers displayed their wares outside their premises by way of advertisement. Shops stayed open until late in the evening. In those days the owners lived over the shop and the town centre was a much more closely knit community than it is today.

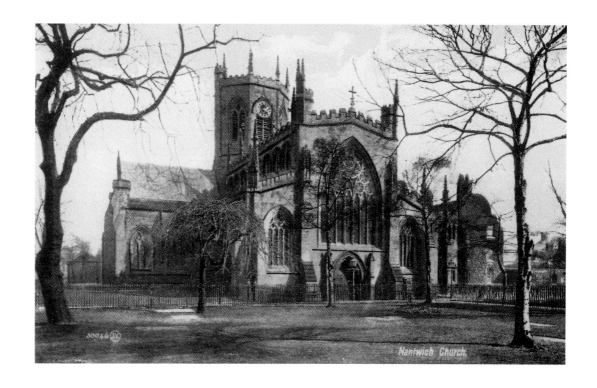

1. The jewel in Nantwich's crown is St. Mary's parish church. This view gives a clear picture of the west end as seen from across the graveyard in the days when the churchyard was surrounded by iron railings.

The Aqueduct, Nantwich.

2. Traveling eastwards from Chester the visitor might be deceived to think this picture shows a West Gate to a walled town. Instead, a narrow boat or barge can be seen crossing the aqueduct of the Shropshire Union Canal. Earlier this century much cheese was carried by canal routes northwards to the Mersey, Liverpool and Manchester; southwards to the Midlands of England. Immediately ahead of the aqueduct are Welsh Row (right) and Welshman's Lane (left). Both record the presence long ago of traders from Wales who brought cattle to sell for Nantwich salt.

COTTAGE HOSPITAL, NANTWICH

3. At the beginning of Welshman's Lane stands the building which began life in 1907 as a new Cottage Hospital for the town and neighbourhood. It served until 1971 when it was superseded by Leighton Hospital on the edge of Crewe. The building is now used for commercial purposes.

NTCH. 39   TOLLEMACHE ALMSHOUSES, WELSH ROW, NANTWICH

4. The Wilbraham family, noted for its generosity to Nantwich, can be traced in a number of buildings. Sir Roger Wilbraham, who lived at Dorfold Hall not far from this scene, founded the first almshouses in 1613. They were rebuilt in 1870 by John Tollemache, also of Dorfold Hall and modernised in 1986. The almshouses provided for four poor men from Nantwich and two from Acton (nearby village). Each man was given nearly £3 a year together with one pair of shoes, gown and cap.

5. This row of thatched cottages called Malbank Cottages (1914) gives a good idea of the kind of homes Nantwich people had in the nineteenth century. In the background (right) is the steeple of the grammar school.

NANTWICH GRAMMAR SCHOOL.

6. In 1548 the Guildhall, near St.Mary's church, was disbanded. The premises were adapted to make the first grammar school. The population was then about 2,000. The school continued for over 300 years until in 1860 it moved to the new premises shown here (1916) combining with a charity (Bluecap) school. In 1921 this building was too small. It was replaced by a modern spacious building also in Welsh Row.

7. Although this parade is outside the (second) grammar school, King James I visited the original school near the parish church on August 25th 1617. He stayed the night at Townsend House, the home of Thomas Wilbraham and next day attended church and visited the brine pit and salt works.

8. Townwell House in Regency style of circa 1740 was built on the site of the town's well. It is now an antiques business. The timber-framed house from the seventeenth century is a good example of a gable end which jetties out over the ground floor (1890).

Welsh Row, Nantwich.

9. Turning to face towards the centre of town, the signs of horse-drawn vehicles along the cobbled street remind us that in earlier times it was called Frog Channel because a stream from beyond the aqueduct flowed down the street to the river Weaver. The stream was put into a culvert in 1865. The bridge can be seen (right) below the church tower.

Welsh Row. — **Nantwich.**

10. Nearer to town (left) are former almshouses. The two gables (right) are part of the Savings Bank of 1846. Street gas lighting is seen (1912).

Widows' Almshouses, Nantwich.

11. Built by Thomas Wilbraham in 1637 these three houses are a fine example of timber-framing with heavy window frames and brick infill. As almshouses they provided living quarters for six widows who were given gowns and required to attend church where they received bread. By 1935 the houses were empty and decaying; after 1945 they were restored and turned into the Cheshire Cat Restaurant. The well-worn steps (right) were a mounting block for ladies to mount their horses and sit side-saddle.

12. This painting shows the typical thatched, timber-framed cottages which were near to The Cheshire Cat. They were in First (or Great) Wood Street, Second (or Little) Wood Street and Cross Wood Street — all named after the places where wood was stored for the fires in salt-making.

13. At its peak in 1597 Nantwich had 216 salthouses. Nantwich owes its existence to the making of salt from brine found only twenty feet down in the ground. Several springs have been located along the course of the river Weaver.

Welsh Row, Nantwich.

14. Looking outward from the town bridge (1920). On the left the 'Bass' sign hangs outside the 'Swan with two necks' said to be a corruption from 'two nicks' on the beak denoting ownership. On the right is a butcher's shop from where, the story goes, the butcher came to sharpen his knives on the mounting block (by boys and bicycle) seen on an earlier view and thus accounts for the much worn away steps.

The Bridge, Nantwich.

15. The first bridge here, made of wood was put up in 1389. It is recorded as having four shops on it, that is, open stalls, and also St. Anne's chapel on it or very near it in Welsh Row (left). The bridge was ruined in a flood and replaced in 1623, then with a stone and wood bridge in 1663 helped by Roger Wilbraham. The bridge seen here was erected by William Lightfoot, a local stonemason, in 1803. In the right background is the former Town Hall.

THE WEAVER, NANTWICH.

16. The reverse view from the town bridge (1916). The massive corn/cotton spinning mill which straddled the river at Mill Street. Children from the workhouse or orphanage worked here under an apprentice scheme 1788-1802. The fourth storey was added in 1834. The mill was idle for most of the years between 1846-64. It closed in 1874 over a strike by female workers and then re-opened as a corn mill. The portion on the right was a foundry with a clothing factory above. It was demolished in 1970.

17. Upstream from the mill are these pastoral scenes. The cattle remind us that cheesemaking was a specialty in Cheshire with Cheese Fairs staged in Nantwich.

Mill Fields, Nantwich.

Johnson & Son
Nantwich.

18. Water above this weir was directed (left) to provide power from the water wheel in the mill (1914). The footbridge has been removed, spoiling what would be a very pleasant circular walk.

19. Scene to the right of the weir. The river Weaver winds its way through the flat valley (1905).

RIVER WEAVER, NANTWICH.   HILL'S GLOSSY PHOTO SERIES.

20. When rowing was a popular recreation (1905).

21. With such a flat valley it is to be expected that heavy rain will result in flooded fields and then floodwater might spill into nearby roads. The cow seems unconcerned! (1903).

94982.J.V.

THE BRIDGE AND HIGH STREET, NANTWICH.

22. Back at the town bridge, looking along lower High Street (1920). On the left is the Town Hall built too near to the river. It was erected in 1868 and paid for by public subscriptions. It contained: Corn Exchange, Assembly Hall (1,000 seats), two committee rooms, library, hall-keeper's residence. By 1945 the building was considered unsafe but left standing for another twenty years before it was demolished to make way for an inner ring road.

High Street, Nantwich

23. This scene is the junction of High Street (foreground), Oat Market (right) and Swine Market (left). High Street continues left to the scene on the previous postcard. Note street gas lights attached to buildings (1908).

Swine Market, Nantwich, 1905

Eustace A. Thompson

24. The White Lion on the corner of Wall Lane and Swine Market. The latter was also known as Beast Market. This is approximately where Woolworth's store stands today.

Wall Lane, Nantwich, 1907. Evacuator A. Philpson

25. Wall Lane extended from Swine Market to Snow Hill. In this area was Lightfoot's Stone Yard. Lightfoot family built the town bridge (1803) and the Beam bridge on the northern edge of the town. Long ago this lane would have led to some of the saltworks. Later it became a centre for the tanning trade.

26. This is the reverse view of No.23 looking up from lower High Street (right) and Swine Market (left) into the middle section of High Street (1906). The Regency Cycle Stores is now an estate agents. The tall building (centre) is Stretch and Harlock's, drapers.

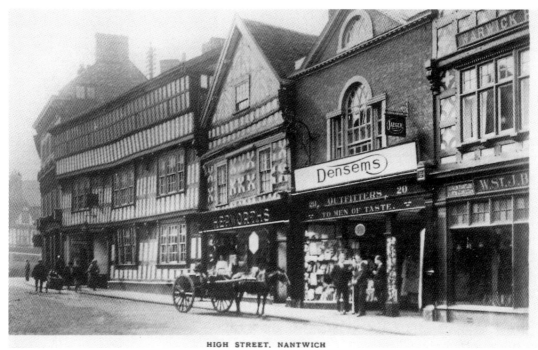

HIGH STREET. NANTWICH

27. This is perhaps the best group of historic buildings. From left to right: The Crown Inn (1584); draper's, outfitter's, draper's. Densem's had once been The Griffin Inn (1927).

The Crown Hotel, Nantwich.

28. The Crown (and Sceptre) Inn, rebuilt after the Great Fire of 1583. It was once a coaching inn on the route from London to Chester. It has a large assembly room with minstrels' gallery. The top storey was once a gallery in which the gentry staying at the inn could take some exercise without venturing into the muddy or dusty street below (1910).

29. A view from 1900 when the timbers of the Crown Inn were hidden behind plaster.

30. A painting made in one of the courtyards somewhere behind High Street (1908).

31. High Street as it was in the 1860s. The Buttermarket (centre) was built in 1720, partly fell in 1737 and 1759. It housed the Booth Hall or Court Hall. Along with the adjoining properties it was demolished about 1868 to make way for the Square to be created. This opened up the view of the church seen in No.1. The background store is Stretch and Harlock's drapers.

Old Houses, The Square, Nantwich

32. Between the Vaults Inn (left) and George Bros. is Castle Street leading to the castle mound and the river. George Bros. is a well preserved example of late sixteenth timber-framed building with much close studding, carvings and ornamentation. These and other buildings in High Street have been carefully restored in recent years.

NANTWICH.

33. A similar view shows how the Square has opened up the street (compare with No.31). An open top omnibus can be seen (1905). This area is now pedestrianised and some trees have been planted and flower troughs added to the Square.

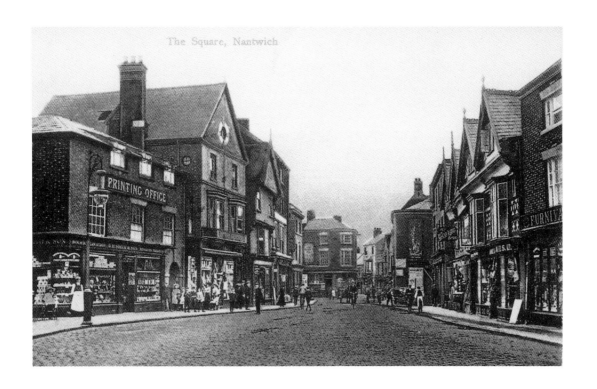

34. High Street seen from Stretch and Harlock's (1906). In the background is Pillory Street (right) and Hospital Street (left).

The Square, Nantwich.

35. Two changes from the previous view may be noted. In the background a new department-type store has been erected (1911) on the corner of Pillory Street and Hospital Street. W.H. Smith & Son (left) have given their premises a facelift in mock timber style.

36. This extensive view (1930s) shows the Square and the main hub of the town. On the left is the First World War memorial (1921) and alongside W.H. Smith & Son is Church Walk leading to the west door of the church.

COPYRIGHT
NTCH. 15

PARISH CHURCH. (A) NANTWICH

37. Churchyardside (south). This block was erected in 1864. The bollards are now included in the list of Listed Buildings and are to be preserved.

38. With the Square opened up, a central position was available for the war memorial to be set among the railings surrounding the churchyard.

39. The visit of H.R.H. Prince of Wales, 1926. The Prince laid a wreath at the war memorial. Since then the railings have been removed and the memorial is almost central in a pedestrianised Square and High Street.

40. The first motor omnibus began service between Nantwich and Crewe in 1905. The gentry seem to prefer the upper deck!

WE ARE GOING
THE PACE AT   NANTWICH

In our fine motor car, we can go near and far
   The sights of the country admiring,
And we carry behind, 'neath the motor confined,
   The beauties we think most inspiring.

41. Under the bonnet of this 1920s car there is a strip of views of Nantwich.

Market Square. — **Nantwich.**

I feel so disappointed at not being able to come down.

42. Similar to No.34 this view gives a better picture of the 'Queen's Aid House'. Lipton's grocer's and W.H. Smith & Son are to the left (1905).

43. Known as the 'Queen's Aid House' this commemorates the generosity of Queen Elizabeth I in giving Nantwich £1,000 to help rebuild the 140 properties that were burnt to the ground in the Great Fire of December 1583. The wording alongside is taken from the plaques and panel on the front of the building (1928).

QUEEN BESS CAFE.

GOD GRANTE OUR RYAL QUEEN IN ENGLAND LONGE TO RAIGN, FOR SHE HATH PUT HER HELPING HAND TO BILD THIS TOWNE AGAIN.

THOMAS CLEESE MADE THIS WORKE THE YEARE OF OURE LORDE GOD. 1584.

THE SQUARE, NANTWICH.

44. This view (circa 1910) shows the end of Pillory Street where it meets High Street. Stretch and Harlock's is in the background on the Square. On the right is the impressive Edwardian style department store standing on the corner of Pillory Street and Hospital Street. On the left are: Sterling's footwear; Peake, baker, and behind the horse and trap on the site of No.6 once lived Mrs. Elizabeth Milton, widow of the blind poet John Milton, author of *Paradise Lost*.

Pillory Street, Nantwich.

45. The reverse of No.44 looking south (1920). Where a tree can be seen there is a replica of the pillory. On the right is The White Horse Inn. The tall building on the left was once the Cocoa House (1897) where a cup of tea, coffee or cocoa, or a bowl of soup could be bought and newspapers were available for reading. There was a room set aside for ladies. Penny tokens were accepted. It opened in 1878 in premises across the road. This was the temperance challenge to the public houses. Beyond, the three tall windows indicate the building for Nantwich Free Library (1888) to mark Queen Victoria's Diamond Jubilee. It now houses Nantwich Museum.

46. This quiet lane runs off Pillory Street (1907). The timber-framed cottages were at the far end adjoining Barker Street. There was a blacksmith's shop and almshouses for four poor men and their wives. The latter was set up in 1722 and survived for 250 years.

47. Near the junction of Barker Street and Mill Street stood this chapel used by the Baptists from 1725. Mrs. Elizabeth Milton attended services here and was buried nearby. Here the building is the Salvation Army's Barracks. (circa 1905.)

Barker st Nantwich.

Evacuates A. Phipson 1907

48. Barker means tannery and in this street tanning used to be carried on. This timber-framed building with brick infill looks much the same today (1907).

49. Also in Barker Street these cottages have been replaced by fine Georgian houses making a notable architectural group in a quiet backwater at a point opposite the scene in Love Lane (No.46). (1907).

SHREWBRIDGE ROAD, NANTWICH.

50. Before the inner ring road was built, Barker Street continued southward and ran into Shrewbridge Road. This long terrace extends to the level crossing in the distance. (The town still has three level crossings.) The backs of the houses look out on to the fields by the river bank (1926).

Shrewbridge Road, Nantwich

51. Beyond the level crossing a row of large semi-detached houses face on to Brookfield Park with playing fields and children's play area. The view from the rear of the houses is towards the riverside (1917).

Wellington Road, Nantwich

52. Somewhat similar houses are to be seen in Wellington Road which is a continuation of Pillory Street across another level crossing. Further south, on both sides, are large elegant houses occupied by professional people. The view at the back is also on to Brookfield Park (1916).

BRINE BATHS HOTEL, NANTWICH

27.9 - 9.10.05.

53. Views from the 1900-1910 period. In the introduction and later it was recorded that Nantwich owes its prominence to the production of salt from brine bubbling up out of the ground…

BRINE BATH HOTEL. NANTWICH

54. Shrewbridge Hall and eighty acres had passed through several hands (currier, mill owner, boot and shoe manufacturer, speculator) in the eighteenth and nineteenth centuries before a company was formed to create the Brine Baths Hotel (1892-1932). The grounds lay between Shrewbridge Road, Park Road and Audlem Road...

THE BROAD WALK. BRINE BATHS HOTEL NANTWICH

55. There was a lake, lawns, gardens, tennis, croquet, a walled garden and several glasshouses and a fruit garden. The aim was to turn Nantwich into a spa town comparable with Harrogate, Buxton, Droitwich. It was claimed to be superior to Bad Kissingen or Carlsbad…

BRINE BATHS HOTEL, NANTWICH.—THE LIBRARY.

56. There were 54 bedrooms; eight baths for different types of complaint; and a library. Brine was pumped up from a spring only a short distance away. The experiment failed and Nantwich lost a valuable asset…

MAIN PATH IN INNER GARDEN, BRINE BATHS HOTEL, NANTWICH

57. After the sale in 1932 the buildings suffered a slow decline, serving as accommodation for the Women's Auxiliary Air Force, then as a convalescent home until about 1958. Everything was demolished to make way for a new housing estate.

Broad Lane, Nantwich.

58. In the wooded background would be seen the Brine Baths Hotel. (1905) These detached houses mark the southern limit of large houses on this side of Nantwich. To the left now stands Brine Leas County High School.

CREWE Rd NANTWICH

59. Retracing one's steps along Wellington Road and Hospital Street we come to the junction of London Road and Crewe Road. This view (1904) shows terraced red-brick houses very similar to the ones seen in Shrewbridge Road (no.50) except that the Crewe Road ones have bay windows upstairs as well as down.

60. In the foreground is London Road with an earlier building for the Leopard Inn (right). Beyond is Hospital Street with the exterior of the mid-eighteenth, ivy-covered house, The Rookery. (1900.)

Hospital Street and The Rookery, Nantwich

61. The third house on the left is built on the site of St. Nicholas hospice founded in 1093 to provide alms and shelter and say prayers for travellers. (1907.)

Churche's Mansion, Nantwich.

62. Opposite The Rookery and at the end of Hospital Street stands Churche's Mansion, built in 1577. London Road is to the left.

Churche's Mansion, A. D. 1577. Nantwich.

Thomas Clease made this worke anno dmi mccccclxxbii,
in the xbiii yere of the reate of our noble queene elezabeth.

63. This shows that Thomas Cleese built this attractive mansion for Richard Church and his wife Margery. The view (1907) shows the time when the house was used for a girls' school. The richness of the house is seen in the profusion of timber and the quantity of decorative woodwork…

CHURCHE'S MANSION, NANTWICH, 1577

64. The Mansion was nearly demolished in 1930 but was saved by a local doctor and his wife who restored the building as their personal 'folly'. Some of the windows have been enlarged and leaded panes incorporated....

CHURCHE'S MANSION, NANTWICH, 1577

65. Note the very wide floor boards and the continuous wood paneling.

66. From Churche's Mansion our journey continues into the background of this view, along Hospital Street, to reach the building on the left. This is Sweet Briar Hall built about 1450. These two views show the Hall when the timber-framing was hidden by pebble dash... (1900).

Sweet Briar Hall, Nantwich.

67. The building fell into partial decay but was saved at the last moment. The front garden and railings were removed; the pebble dash removed to reveal an excellent example of timber-frame construction including decorative pieces to make a wealthy man's home.

NTCH 4 NANTWICH, HOSPITAL STREET.

68. From Sweet Briar Hall inwards Hospital Street is a thriving business centre with many shops and services. A timber framed building stands on the corner of Church Lane (centre); behind it is the portico entrance to the Lamb Hotel: founded circa 1554 as a tavern; burnt down in the Great Fire (1583); served as headquarters for the Parliamentary forces in the Civil War and the battle of Nantwich (1644); and rebuilt 1861. It was much frequented in the 1920s by farmers and others on market days when the yard and nearby streets would be filled with conveyances.

Hospital St. — **Nantwich.**

69. Two views of the beginning of Hospital Street. Right: this one is of about 1890. High Street is in the background. Above: a 1914 view showing that this old house has been replaced by a pseudo-timber-framed building (left). Next to it is the Lamb Hotel. Beyond that is the entrance to Church Lane and, on the corner, the timber-framed building of No.68 when the timbers were hidden under paint or plaster.

Dysart Buildings, Nantwich.

70. Turning into Church Lane the walk continues round the outside of the church to reach this view. Dysart Buildings (1778/79) are nine fine town houses with long gardens. The land was owned by the 5th Lord Dysart as inherited from his great grandfather who married Grace Wilbraham in 1680. The gaslit passage is Monk's Lane, a reminder that long ago, before the Reformation, monks who officiated at the church came this way to cultivate their plots of land. On the right is the 1842 Congregational chapel and school. The chapel has been converted into several luxury homes.

Johnson series.　　　　　　　　BAPTIST CHAPEL, NANTWICH.

71. From Church Lane and Churchyardside we turn into Market Street with the Market Hall, a one-time school and a former cinema. This Baptist chapel was used after the Baptists left Barker Street (1905). All has been replaced by a modern chapel for the United Reform Church.

SIR E. WRIGHT'S ALMHOUSES, NANTWICH

72. Turning next into Beam Street a short walk brings us to the restored Crewe/Wright/Hope alms-houses, an amalgamation of three bequests (1975). Sir Edmund Wright (1573-) was another of Nantwich's benefactors. His almshouses (1634) were originally in London Road (as on No.60). He provided for six single Nantwich men, especially if named Wright, over 50 years of age. Each was given a shirt, a pair of stockings and a pair of shoes on each Christmas day, as well as two shillings (10p.) a quarter. They wore a long, brown overcoat and a distinctive hat.

ALL SAINTS. NANTWICH.

73. After the cholera epidemic of 1849 the churchyard was closed for burials and a new cemetery opened on the northern edge of Nantwich off Barony Road. All Saints chapel was built in 1884. (1913)

NANTWICH—
The rides about here are
most enjoyable.

The Introduction.

74. This postcard is applicable to Nantwich which is surrounded on all sides by the Cheshire Plain and fairly level roads for pleasant cycling (1910).

—✦ NANTWICH OLD BAND. ✦—

T. Sadler, junr.   S. Parkes.   T. Hassall.   W. Hassall.   J. Benbow.   T. Gilbert.
C. Hassall, senr.   A. Parkes.   W. Gilbert.   T. Betley.   T. Sadler, senr.

75. The Band in 1904. It continued until 1939.

Nantwich Church.

THE DEVIL & LANDLADY, NANTWICH CHURCH.

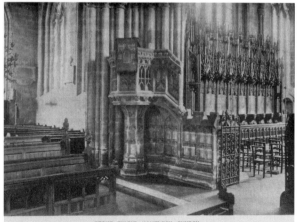

STONE PULPIT, NANTWICH CHURCH.

76. Returning to the town centre we look again at the magnificent church. Behind the stone pulpit are to be seen the beautifully carved choir stalls. The seats carry fascinating misericords depicting ways of life in medieval times.

This gargoyle shows the Devil seizing a landlady found stealing money from a pot.

St. Mary's parish church, Nantwich, in winter.